52 More Weeks of Gratitude:

Thank Your Way to Happiness

Lisa Ryan, MBA

Grategy®

http://www.grategy.com

Table of Contents

Welcome!... 1

Week 1: Increasing the World's Happiness 2

Week 2: Doing the Things That Others Won't 4

Week 3: What's Holding You Back?... 6

Week 4: What Are You Built For?.. 8

Week 5: The Key to a Happy Life.. 10

Week 6: "Glass Half-full" People... 12

Week 7: Every Difficulty has an Opportunity....................... 14

Week 8: See Your Days for What They Are........................... 16

Week 9: Gratitude Involves a Conscious Choice 18

Week 10: Do the Right Thing at the Right Time 20

Week 11: Putting Your Appreciation into Words 22

Week 12: Don't waste time.. 24

Week 13: A Renaissance Awaits You 26

Week 14: Kindness, Beauty, and Truth................................... 28

Week 15: Attitude is Contagious 30

Week 16: Gratitude is to Marriage as Oil is to an Engine... 31

Week 17: Smile at the Check-Out Clerk 33

Week 18: Getting Fired Up After Getting Fired 34

Week 19: Delays are not Denials... 36

Week 20: Being Willing to Receive 38

Week 21: Your Success Depends on Your Persistence 40

Week 22: Relishing Your Gifts 42

Week 23: Asking is Only Part of the Equation 44

Week 24: The essence of all art, is gratitude 46

Week 25: Be the Change You Wish to See in The World ... 48

Week 26: The Greatest Danger Lies Not in Setting Your
Aim too High 50

Week 27: Understanding the Reality of the Everyday 52

Week 28: Good Works are Links That Form a Chain of
Love 54

Week 29: It's Always Too Early to Quit 56

Week 30: Appreciate what you have 58

Week 31: Life's "Calculator Carriers" 60

Week 32: Risk Anything! 62

Week 33: - Sixty Days from Now 64

Week 34: The Best Minute 66

Week 35: Be Nice to EVERYONE! 68

Week 36: Take a Risk - and Act 70

Week 37: Creating a Vision for Tomorrow 72

Week 38: Be Careful What You Wish For 74

Week 39: Week - Nothing Can Stop You 76

Week 40: The Real Winner in Life 78

Week 41: Nothing is Good or Bad 80

Week 42: A First Rate Version of Yourself 82

Week 43: Concentrate on the Good 84

Week 44: Self-Help versus Shelf-Help 86

Week 45: Be grateful for your problems 88

Week 46: Asking for What You Want 90

Week 47: - Life's Free Gifts 92

Week 48: Sincere Words of Praise 94

Week 49: Leaving the World a Better Place 96

Week 50: Who You Are and Who You May Be 98

Week 51: Regretting the Things You Haven't Done 100

Week 52: Escaping the Pressures of Mainstream Media ... 102

Congratulations! 104

About Lisa Ryan 106

Other Books from Lisa Ryan: 108

Let's Keep in Touch 110

Welcome!

52 More Weeks of Gratitude is a compilation of my second year's writings of "Gratitude Thought of the Week." You can read it from cover to cover, or choose to open the book to a random page and experience a unique way of looking at the world through the eyes of appreciation.

Receive your own "Gratitude Thought of the Week" by visiting www.grategy.com

Week 1: Increasing the World's Happiness

"You have it easily in your power to increase the sum total of this world's happiness now. How? By giving a few words of sincere appreciation to someone who is lonely or discouraged. Perhaps you will forget tomorrow the kind words you say today, but the recipient may cherish them over a lifetime."

Dale Carnegie

Because our words have a profound impact - one that can be a very positive or negative consequence - it's important to be aware of what we say to others, as. Often, we are not aware of how our words hurt.

At the beginning of my career, I worked with a woman who told me that I was "permanent potential." I interpreted this statement to mean that I had a lot of potential, but I would never actually amount to anything. It hurt. Looking back, I realize there are many reasons she would have uttered that phrase. She may have said it in frustration, or to inspire me to get better, or she may have just said it for no particular reason at all. Chances are she doesn't remember saying it. However, I remembered.

Like mom used to say, "If you can't say anything nice, don't say anything at all." Consciously consider ALL of the words that come out of your mouth today. If you need to make a negative remark, criticize the action - not the person. People may do stupid things, but they are not idiots.

Your words of affirmation not only bring somebody up when they're feeling down, but others will cherish your words for a lifetime.

PS - Tell someone you are proud of them today.

Week 2: Doing the Things That Others Won't

"You must do the things today that others will not do so that you can have the things tomorrow that others will not have."

Anonymous

Remember the days, early in your career when you thought to have it all meant a cool title, a business card, and your own office with a door. When you reached those goals, life was grand. After a while, the title, card, and office are no longer enough, and you're ready for your "next." What happens then?

One of my first jobs was at a placement agency, "selling secretaries." It turned out to be a disaster, but I liked sales, I was learning a lot, and I persisted. For several years, I failed miserably in sales. It wasn't until my fourth sales job that I experienced success. Finally, I enjoyed what I did AND had all the perks of the successful rep. Life was grand once again. Persistence pays off.

Consider this: Jack Canfield contacted 144 publishers with his *Chicken Soup for the Soul* book before he finally got one to accept it. Where do you think Jack would be if he had stopped after sending it to 100 publishers? As my friend Dahmia says, "Persistence is the name of the game and the more experience we have, the better choices we make - persistence doesn't work if you're digging a post hole in the wrong location - deeper isn't going to make it better."

Be grateful today for your persistence. If you're not exactly where you want to be in your life, but you're taking baby steps towards your goal - you'll get there. Enjoy the journey and ultimately you'll reach your destination.

PS - Others may not understand your journey, its ok. Persist anyway.

Week 3: What's Holding You Back?

"It's not what you ARE that holds you back; it's what you think you're NOT."

Denis Waitley

In the movie, "The Keeper of the Keys," author Judith Wright talks about her experiences with writing end of life stories for people. She found that people have three regrets: 1) they didn't risk enough; 2) they didn't reflect enough, and 3) they didn't give back enough. Consider how you can become more of who you are by tackling these three regrets NOW.

Risk more. When people reach the end of the road on this planet, and they start to look back on their lives, they are more likely regret the things that they did NOT do, versus the risks they took. What do you dream about doing? What's on your bucket list? Choose one thing this month, and go for it. No matter what happens, in the end, you'll be glad you gave it a try.

Reflect more. Take the time to meditate. Max Bolka shares the importance of meditation in "The Keeper of the Keys" as a way to turn one's life around. Just ten minutes a day can make a huge difference (If all you have is five minutes - start there).

Give more. When we are feeling down, one of the best things we can do is help someone else. Write a check to your favorite charity. Read to an elderly person. Run some errands for a harried neighbor. Send a letter of appreciation to someone you love.

Will you look back at a "life well lived" or will you have wished that you would have done more? Take action today; you won't regret it.

PS - "I wish I would have" are the five of the saddest words in the world.

Week 4: What Are You Built For?

"A ship in port is safe, but that's not what ships are built for."

Grace Hopper

At a recent networking event, I met a young woman who lost her job and was desperately seeking her next position. As we talked, she spoke enthusiastically and with a passion for what she loved doing. Her face lit up when she talked about her dream career. I asked her, "So, why don't you just start your own business doing exactly that?"

And the excuses began: "I'm a single mom. There's not enough work to keep me employed. Other people have a bad image of 'consultants'" and so on. We spoke for a few minutes longer, and when she saw I wasn't going to commiserate with her plight or let her off the hook for not following her bliss, she went on to find a more sympathetic ear.

Often, life throws us a curveball to see how committed we are to making our dreams come true. Yes, it takes hard work to start your own business, and it can be incredibly frustrating at times, but the payoff in finding your purpose makes it all worthwhile.

A friend once told me about the two most important days of a person's life - the day you are born, and the day you find out why. Think about one thing that you can do TODAY that's just for you. You never know where your path will lead you when you discover your life purpose.

PS - Don't die with your music still inside you. The very thing that lights you up will change your life - as well as the lives of others.

Week 5: The Key to a Happy Life

"Gratefulness is the key to a happy life that we hold in our hands, because if we are not grateful, then no matter how much we have we will not be happy -- because we will always want to have something else or something more."

David Steindl-Rast

Do you find yourself always in a state of "When?" You know, "When I close this big deal," "When I meet the love of my life," "When my kids go off to college." etc. Are you "when-ing" yourself away from your highest and best self?

Isn't it true that we tend to teach the lessons we need to learn for ourselves? Sure enough, this is one that I have worked on for a while now. It took time for me to recognize that "when" will happen soon enough, and now is the time to enjoy this remarkable journey. My life became better with that awareness.

When you take the time to meditate, to pray or reflect, or to take time in self-care, you realize that everything you need is right here, right now. You can't change the past and the future isn't here yet. NOW is a gift - and that's why they call it the PRESENT. Life comes at you fast - enjoy the ride.

PS - When I get done with this blog post, I'm treating myself to a bowl of ice cream. Ok, that's a good "when!" :-)

Week 6: "Glass Half-full" People

"Hang around optimists. Refresh your own psyche and spirit by socializing with people who don't just see the glass half full but are willing to share that glass with you. They understand they'll gain so much more."

Denis Waitley

Isn't that a nice thought - to not only hang out with people who see the glass as half-full but those who are willing to share the glass with you? It goes to show you; there is always enough.

Do you have people in your life that suck the soul out of your being every time you are around them? No matter what you do, you feel unacknowledged, unappreciated, and unloved by these people. Sure, they may put on a "happy face" which adds to your confusion, making you feel like it's you. Chances are it's not - these relationships are destructive and will keep you stuck.

Make a conscious decision to remove "energy vampires" from your life, or at least strictly limit your time with them. When you are working on creating a bigger, better you, others may not like it. They won't feel comfortable, and they feel like you are leaving them behind. "Oh, you're too good for us, right?" When they try to bring you down - stand your ground.

There are plenty of people that love and support you for who you are now and for who you are becoming. If you don't know who they are, go out and meet them.

Have you met someone that is a kindred spirit? Call them up and invite them out to coffee. Learn as much as you can about them. When you are interested in them, they will be interested in you. Build your network of influential supporters and experience the power of the presence of positive people.

PS - The more you associate with people who see the glass as half-full, the fuller your life becomes.

Week 7: Every Difficulty has an Opportunity

"The difference between an obstacle and an opportunity is our attitude towards it. Every opportunity has a difficulty, and every difficulty has an opportunity."

J .Sidlo Baxter

"I see no reason why your dad can't live on his own." When I heard this phrase uttered by the social worker who assessed my father, I experienced a broad range of emotions. I was surprised because it was not what I was expecting. I was upset because I wasn't sure it was right for him to do. I was proud of my dad for working so hard to be able to go back home again. I was afraid because I want to be able to keep my father safe. I was glad to see him so darn happy. Most of all, I was confused - so many emotions to deal with, and no idea what was going to happen. Ultimately, I had to find opportunities to find gratitude in the midst of so many obstacles.

I'm grateful for the Guardian Medical Alert system that my dad has to keep him safe. I'm thankful for the automated medication dispenser gives him what he needs to stay healthy. I appreciate my husband who was instrumental in helping me move dad back home. Most of all, I'm very glad I have a father that loves and appreciates me and our time together.

What obstacles are you facing in your life right now? Take a moment and consider the good things that have happened as a result of a severe event in your life, and you'll realize how blessed you are. If you're in the throes of a difficult situation right now, know that in time, it will be easier to find something to appreciate about the event. In the meantime, pick just ONE THING you can be thankful for about it.

PS - Even if you're grateful for just "another day above ground," it's a good start...

Week 8: See Your Days for What They Are

"I see now, that the moments and fragments of my life return to the soil, like the seeds of a flower. The bigger the day, the better the seed. I know that precious few will take root and grow into something lasting, but I see my days for what they truly are, not one moment or fragment too soon."

Markus Pierson

On October 6, 2012, I said my final goodbye to my ex-husband, Jeff, twice. After a long battle with pancreatic and liver cancer, Jeff decided he no longer wished to fight the disease; he wanted to be out of pain. Our first conversation was short and sweet. After I had hung up the phone, I asked myself if I said everything I wanted to say. The answer was "no," so I called him back. We talked until we were complete. Jeff passed away on October 21st.

Jeff was in my life for 34 years. Although our marriage didn't work out, we maintained our friendship. We shared plenty of good and created a lot of fun memories together, and for all of this, I am incredibly grateful. I would not be who I am if Jeff was not with me.

I'm also glad I had the opportunity to say everything I wanted to say to him on our call. No regrets. Nothing left unsaid. I realize that not many people have the honor of this kind of expression, and I don't take this blessing lightly.

Take a moment today to share, from your heart, your feelings about a loved one to them. Don't wait for the eulogy to express your feelings about a person; that individual needs to hear your positive words of love and affirmation while they still can.

PS - Words count. You make a difference by what you choose to say every day.

Week 9: Gratitude Involves a Conscious Choice

"Gratitude as a discipline involves a conscious choice...It is amazing how many occasions present themselves in which I can choose gratitude instead of a complaint."

Henri J. M. Nouwen

W Mitchell is one of the most amazing and inspirational people on the planet. If you're not familiar with him, check out: http://www.wmitchell.com/. The Cliff Notes version of Mitchell's story is that he was in a motorcycle accident in which he suffered burns over 65% of his body. If that wasn't bad enough, four years later, he was in a plane crash and became a paraplegic. Did he complain and wither away? No, he ran for mayor of his town on the slogan, "Not just another pretty face," was elected and went on to save a mountain. He travels around the world, sharing the message that "it's not what happens to you, it's what you do with it." Mitchell is also one of the nicest, most approachable, and genuine people I have ever met.

Mitchell says that there were 10,000 things that he could do before his accident. After his accident, he could still do 9,000 of those things. He figured, why should he complain about the things he couldn't do when he could focus on the myriad things he still could accomplish.

Although my story is not even close to Mitchell's, I know that I still have to make a conscious choice to get to gratefulness when life throws me a curve ball. It's often difficult, but my daily gratitude practice helps.

What about you? How easy is it for you to get to gratitude in challenging situations? Find three to five things you appreciate every day. By strengthening your gratitude muscle, you will find it easier to choose to praise instead of to complain. It works.

PS - If your story is not going the way you want, make the choice to create a different ending.

Week 10: Do the Right Thing at the Right Time

"I try to do the right thing at the right time. They may just be little things, but usually, they make the difference between winning and losing."

Kareem Abdul-Jabbar

We've all seen the sign, "You break it, you buy it." While shopping in a local consignment story, I broke something. It didn't just break, it shattered - a loud, reverberating crash of a crystal lamp that found the wrong end of my purse in an otherwise empty shop. Ugh, no getting out of this one. I have to admit; I didn't want to pay for something I wasn't taking home. However, when I asked myself the question, "What's the right thing to do?" There was only one answer. I handed the owner the money for the lamp, apologizing for my mess. She was relieved and grateful, saying, "If it were my lamp, I would just let it go, but since this is a customer's item, I can't. Thanks so much for taking care of this."

My friend Chris was on the other side of a consignment store, "I was a potter who made sculptural pots by hand. I had a large one in a consignment store that someone broke. The owners of the store called me to pick up the pieces. They did not offer to reimburse me in any way, so while there I picked up all the other pieces of my work that were on consignment with them. The interesting aftermath was that they went out of business soon after this incident."

When you have the opportunity to do the right thing, take it. You make a difference to the person you help, and you increase your sense of self-worth. The lesson is more valuable than the price.

PS - Do enough of the little things, and it will prepare you for the big challenges that life hands you.

Week 11: Putting Your Appreciation into Words

"Appreciation can make a day, even change a life. Your willingness to put it into words is all that is necessary."

Margaret Cousins

A little more than a year after my father's stroke, a social worker assessed him to see if he could live on his own and if he was able to drive. He had permission to live on his own, but he did not pass the driving assessment. (I have to admit, I was relieved.) If you have elderly parents or grandparents, you know that losing their ability to drive, in essence, their independence; it is one of the hardest things for them. My dad was no exception.

Knowing that he would be upset, I invited him to a networking event where I was speaking. Several people signed up for this event who had retired from Huntington Bank, and my father knew them from his 30-year tenure there. My dad put aside his feelings of sadness and reconnected with old friends. He radiated joy and thanked everyone from the hosts of the meeting to the servers of the food.

So what do you do when life brings you down? Do you choose to wallow or can you move past it, if only for a little while, and pay attention to the good things in your life?

Just for today, try telling yourself, "I'm going to take a break from my negativity and look for what's positive in my situation for the next (insert number) minutes." When the time is up, you can go back to wallowing, or you may find that you don't need to. Give yourself permission to be okay with either option. The chances are that by taking a break, you'll find that you changed your state enough to get out of the funk and move on to a happier place.

PS - As my friend Jacci, a cancer survivor, said, "Life may come at you fast - but what can you do to get past the curveballs of life? Choose gratitude."

Week 12: Don't waste time

"If you love life, don't waste time, for time is what life is made of."

Bruce Lee

"Hi, my name is Lisa Ryan, and I am an email-aholic." "Hi, Lisa." Did you ever sit down at the computer for "five minutes" to take care of your emails and find yourself still dealing with them FOUR HOURS LATER? Email, if not handled correctly, eats away a good portion of your day and is a HUGE time-waster.

During a trip to Niagara-on-the-Lake, I "disconnected" for the weekend. It is very refreshing not to be available to the world 24/7. I focused my time and my energy entirely on my husband, and we had a wonderful time on our getaway. (And, believe it or not, I didn't miss ANYTHING by not answering my phone or email while away).

When I related that story to my friend Traci, she shared that she and her husband disconnect on a regular basis. I thought, "You mean I don't have to go to Canada to experience the pure pleasure of personal connection instead of a life-interrupting internet connection? What a concept!" My husband and I are going to implement this simple idea and "get-away" more often.

Yes, email is an important communication tool. However, take the time to smell the roses, to personally interact with others, and to fully enjoy your life while you are still on the planet. After all, no one has ever said on their deathbed, "I wish I would have spent more time checking email."

PS - For starters, pick one day - disconnect from technology, and spend quality time with someone you love. I'd love to hear your results.

Week 13: A Renaissance Awaits You

"A renaissance awaits you, if only you apply the pearls of wisdom you already know."

Markus Pierson

You have a lifetime of wisdom stored in your heart and your head. Sometimes your insight is gained from your mistakes, and other times your knowledge is acquired by learning from the tribulations of others. When you take the time to listen to your inner guidance, you choose the right path at the right time.

On the other hand, there's outer wisdom, consisting of stories and anecdotes that we believe to be true. What happens when those pearls of wisdom we already "know," are wrong? Recently I came across several interesting tidbits which disproved beliefs I have held for a long time.

The idea that: "It takes 21 days to form a habit" was uncovered during a study of amputees. Physicians found that it took an amputee 21 days to stop experiencing the phantom pain of the removed limb. Research has shown that it takes 66 days to form a habit. (Yes, I liked 21 days better too!)

"We only use 10% of our brain." In fact, we use all of our brain, even while sleeping. We use only a small percentage of our MENTAL POTENTIAL - and the number is not confirmed to be 10%.

"People are auditory, visual or kinesthetic learners." There is no research to support learning styles. We all learn differently, based on our ability, background knowledge, interests.

What does all of this have to do with gratitude? I'm grateful that I'm open to learning new information. I value those that conduct research and make it available for us to share. And I appreciate the reminder in this quote that I DO have wisdom, and often the best person I can listen to is ME! What wisdom will you share with yourself today?

PS - Meditating is the single best way to go to the heart of what you know. Go into the silence and listen for your innate intelligence to come through.

Week 14: Kindness, Beauty, and Truth

"The ideals that have lighted my way and, time after time, have given me new courage to face life cheerfully have been Kindness, Beauty, and Truth."

Albert Einstein

We have many opportunities throughout the day to experience kindness, beauty, and truth - yet how often do we miss these occasions because we are focusing on the unkind, the ugly and the untrue?

Kindness: On our way to Cedar Point, we stopped to pick up some Dramamine (for my husband, of course). I ran into the store while Scott waited in the car. A couple with a cart massively full of groceries was in front of me. I smiled and asked if I could go before them as I "had only one item and was paying with cash." Not only did they let me through, but we also struck up a conversation, and they wished us a fun day. This couple gave me a small, but very much appreciated act of kindness that started the day on a good note.

Beauty: As we sat in our backyard late one afternoon, a family of deer came for a visit including two moms and three babies - still with their spots. Instead of shooing them away because of the damage they have done to our yard already, we just enjoyed these gentle, beautiful creatures.

Truth seems elusive, as we try to sort through the vast amounts of information every day. (After all, if it's on the internet, it's true, right?) I find that when I take the time to go into the silence and meditate, I can find my truth, and my days are better because of it.

What can you do TODAY to find kindness, beauty, and truth in your life?

PS - It's the little blessings that bring us the greatest joy - when we take the time to notice them.

Week 15: Attitude is Contagious

"Attitude is contagious! What are you passing around?"
Kay Baker

Ali shares what happens when you choose to have a great attitude: "I was thinking about how stressed I am, and how there's simply not enough time with a career, two kids, and a stay-at-home husband in school full-time.

"I decided to do something nice for someone, and when I brought a smile to their face, my stress disappeared. I went to a doctor appointment, and an elderly gentleman opened the exterior door of the building for me and said: "Well get in there." So I walked in, thanked him, and proceeded to open the interior door of the building for him, look at him and say "Well, now YOU get in there." His face lit up, and so did mine, and we both shared a smile and a laugh."

It's the simple things in life that we do that bring light to the world around us. Look for one small thing that you can do today to make someone smile. I'd love to hear about it.

PS - If you see someone without a smile today, give them one of yours.

Week 16: Gratitude is to Marriage as Oil is to an Engine

"Gratitude is to marriage as oil is to an engine. It needs to be applied liberally and throughout and is of such importance, that a fresh supply must be added regularly to ensure success and longevity."

Matthew Smith

Remember when you started dating your spouse/ significant other? Those were the times when everything he or she did made you smile.

You were thrilled when the phone rang, ecstatic when you heard the doorbell announcing his or her arrival, euphoric to receive a kiss. You felt "butterflies" whenever your loved one was around. Life was good.

Over time, your relationship became comfortable. You still have the same feelings for your loved one, but you don't feel the need to go out of your way like you used to. Maybe you stop doing the little things you used to do because your partner also stopped the surprises that added variety and spice to your relationship. What do you do now that the butterflies are flying in formation?

Add gratitude. Look for specific reasons to thank your spouse. Did you come home from a hard day at work and find dinner waiting for you? Say "Thank you." You may be thinking, "But Lisa, my spouse makes dinner for me all the time. Are you talking about that I have to be thankful every single time?" The simple answer is, "Yes."

As you continue to express your gratefulness, there is a real chance that you will also start to be the recipient of your partner's appreciation. It's a virtuous cycle that will keep your relationship going strong and growing for many years to come.

PS - How about putting a note in their lunch bag or leaving one on the front seat of their car? How about meeting them at the door when they come home with a big smile, a hug, and kiss? It's the little things that count BIG.

Week 17: Smile at the Check-Out Clerk

"When eating bamboo sprouts, remember the man who planted them."

Chinese Proverb

Are you busy? Maybe you're taking on projects, going more places, meeting the people, and trying to get more done than ever before? You know that you're not taking time for yourself, but you don't know how you can change your situation. Unfortunately, you have your blinders on, and as you struggle to get your "stuff" done, you fail to notice the world around you. (Or is it just me?)

Think about the number of times you go into your favorite coffee shop, or fast food restaurant, and barely notice the person behind the counter. How often do you say "Hello" to the custodian in your office? What about the mail person UPS driver? Do you take the time to acknowledge them? Notice them. You have no idea the difference that you make.

A simple act of kindness goes a long way. Make it a point to make eye contact, to say smile and say hello to everyone you come into contact with today. If the line is long at the grocery store, and the clerk seems frazzled, that's an excellent time for you to be kind. She needs your smile more than you need to keep it to yourself.

PS - The best friendships start with a simple, "Hello."

Week 18: Getting Fired Up After Getting Fired

"We deem those happy who from the experience of life have learned to bear its ills without being overcome by them."

Carl Jung

Have you ever been fired? In my life, I have been let go four times, and my life has gotten better each time. Here's what happened the second time.

I was in a job I hated. I would leave work on Friday and be depressed about having to go back to work on Monday. It was that bad. I didn't want to quit my job without having another job, but I was stuck. Then, one Sunday night, I was driving home, and I was not looking forward to going to work in the morning. So I decided to pray.

"Dear God, what should I do? Should I quit my job without another job? Should I just stay put? Please, give me a sign." Well, of course, I looked to the heavens for a shooting star of some other sign, but none came. I went to work the next morning, and as soon as I got there, I was called into the manager's office where she promptly fired me. I was shocked, devastated, and dejected as I cleaned out my belongings and was ushered out without a chance to say "Goodbye" to my co-workers.

I found my boyfriend and told him what happened. He said, "You hated that job, so why not just enjoy the summer?" We were in a drought at the time, and I had an awesome summer! As fall rolled around, I found a job a better job and life went on. It was all part of the journey.

Look back at the times when you've lost a job, or experienced some other unexpected, unpleasant event in your life. Looking back, would you have changed a thing?

PS - Of course, working for yourself is a GREAT way never to have to worry about getting fired again.

Week 19: Delays are not Denials

"Never think that God's delays are God's denials. Hold on; hold fast; hold out. Patience is genius. "

Comte Georges Louis

Every time I see the word "patience," I think of that old cartoon with two buzzards sitting on a tree limb. One of the buzzards says to the other, "Patience my a$$, I'm gonna kill something." That's pretty much how I've always felt about being patient.

As an entrepreneur building a business, it's sometimes difficult to wait until all the stars align and I achieve my goals. I'm excited about what lies ahead, and it tends to make me impatient. I want it all, and, of course, I want it NOW. However, I have found that when I take the time to meditate and visualize my future, everything falls into place in ways that are better than I could have imagined.

Have you ever waited a long time for something to happen in your life, and when it finally occurred, you realized that you didn't take the time to enjoy the journey along the way? Make sure you appreciate the people you meet, the places you go and the things that you learn as you reach and exceed your goals beyond your wildest expectations.

Your day is on its way.

PS - Patience is a gift. Enjoy the ride - even if it feels like you're going well below the speed limit.

Week 20: Being Willing to Receive

"Asking is one-half of the mantra; the other half is being willing to receive. Listen and be ever alert, for when the universe answers, it may be in the language of little synchronicities that guide you toward a solution. Ask knowing that an answer is forthcoming. Then be ever alert to catch it."

D. Trinidad Hunt

At some point in your career, you may decide it's time for a change. I reached that point and decided to leave an inside sales position for an outside sales job. I sent out some resumes and set up an interview for an exciting job in the welding industry.

The morning of my interview, one of my cats had surgery to remove a cancerous tumor. Unfortunately, cancer had spread, and she died on the operating table. I cried up until an hour before the interview, then cleaned myself up and went to meet my future employer, Dale.

The interview went great, and I told Dale that if there were going to be a second interview, it would have to be at night. I explained that I took the day off work because one of my pets died that morning. Dale asked me what I had, and I told him, "It was my cat." He replied, "I'm sorry to hear that, I have four cats." That pretty much sealed the deal. Little synchronicities led me to this position, and I stayed there for six years.

Think about the events that happened in your life as a series of coincidences conspired to work out in unexpectedly brilliant ways. When you listen to your inner voice, pay attention to what is going on around you, and know that your answer is forthcoming. Your answer always shows up.

PS - Of course, it doesn't always happen as quickly or in the ways that we expect it to happen - just know that when you get your answer, it will be perfect.

Week 21: Your Success Depends on Your Persistence

"When I thought I couldn't go on, I forced myself to keep going. My success is based on persistence, not luck."

Estee Lauder

Do you know what you want out of your life? Can you see your future clearly in your mind's eye and know down to the very core of your being that what you're working towards is your life's purpose?

It's easy to progress towards your goals when things are going well when you're "in the flow." You feel great; you're on a "high," and things couldn't be better. Because of your positive momentum, when challenges first happen, you turn on your inner turbo-boosters and plow forward.

However, when it seems nothing is going right, challenges are abounding, and you can't see the light at the end of the tunnel, you may start to question your sanity, your motivations, and whether you should continue down this crazy path.

Start to think of your challenges as just another part of your story. Every delay, mistake and denial is part of what it takes to make your victory stronger and more satisfying than if it happened easily and without trials and tribulations. You are on your way, and your efforts will pay off in ways you may not have imagined. Go for it!

PS - Persistence pays. Slow and steady wins the race - it's all just a matter of time.

Week 22: Relishing Your Gifts

"A person however learned and qualified in his life's work in whom gratitude is absent, is devoid of that beauty of character which makes personality fragrant."

Hazrat Inayat Khan

Isn't it true that some gift-giving experiences are better than others?

Perhaps you can relate to one (or both) of these situations: You give a present to a child - she greedily rips open the package, carelessly takes the gift out of the box, glances at it for a split second and then demands to be bestowed the next present. Do you feel good about your gift-giving experience?

Another child relishes opening each gift. He carefully takes your present out of the box and squeals with delight. The sheer joy of receiving your gift distracts him to the point that he needs to be coaxed to put it to the side and open the next gift. How do you feel about this transaction? Which child would you be more likely to give gifts to in the future?

Isn't it true that many adults are just grown-up versions of these kids? It's much more rewarding when your recipients show heartfelt gratitude for your gift - whether it's your time, your talent, or your presents. When others carelessly toss aside your efforts, it doesn't feel good, and you are less likely to help them in the future.

Remember to express your gratitude early and often. You'll make yourself and others happier, and you will open yourself up to receive more from the presents and presence of others.

PS - Squeal with delight in your gratitude - it's sure to bring a smile!

Week 23: Asking is Only Part of the Equation

"Until we can receive with an open heart, we're never really giving with an open heart. When we attach judgment to receiving help, we knowingly or unknowingly attach judgment to giving help."

Brené Brown

When you set your goals and develop a plan to reach them, it's imperative that you are ready and willing to receive success with awe, humility, and the desire to help.

Why do you want to acknowledge your achievements with awe? Because when you reach a hard-fought goal, you realize how extraordinarily powerful you are. Your accomplishments are a reminder that you have the ability to mold your life into whatever form you want it to take.

Acknowledge your accomplishments with humility. Your humbleness reminds you that you did not do this alone. Express your gratitude to everyone and everything that helped you along your journey.

Lastly, use your successes to help others. You can offer your help in a variety of ways. If additional wealth was part of your accomplishment, give some of it away to benefit others. If your goal was to find a new job, become the best employee, colleague, or mentor you can be. You can support the organization in becoming stronger and more profitable because you work there.

Whatever goal you achieved, accept it with gratitude.

PS - As the late Zig Ziglar once said, "You can get everything you want out of life if you just help enough other people get what they want."

Week 24: The essence of all art, is gratitude

"The essence of all beautiful art, all great art, is gratitude."
Friedrich Nietzsche

With its $350 million in renovations, the Cleveland Museum of Art is a magnificent place. My fondest memories of it, however, are those from my childhood.

We went to the Art Museum A LOT when we were kids. Years later, I figured out the reason we went there so often was that it was somewhere we could go for FREE. Fortunately, we all loved going there - particularly the armor gallery, which is still my favorite place in the museum.

Artistic expression is in our nature, and yet how many times do we neglect our calling to express our talents? Melinda shared, "I just visited the Art Museum with my daughter when she was home from college. What a beautiful renovation. We are so blessed to have such University Circle and all the Arts in Cleveland. Your message inspired me to get out watercolors!"

What do you like to do creatively? Do you write? Paint? Knit? Draw? When was the last time you took the time and allowed yourself to indulge in your own creativity? This week make a point to carve out an hour for yourself to do what you love. Even if you just buy the paints or the canvas, take a baby step to unleash your imagination.

Then schedule uninterrupted time to play and let yourself go. Tell your inner critic to take a hike; you don't need him or her. This time is for YOU and you alone. Enjoy it!

PS - No matter what you create, it is YOUR masterpiece.

Week 25: Be the Change You Wish to See in The World

"You must be the change you wish to see in the world."

Gandhi

Did you ever spend weeks dreading an event because of the people you were going to be "stuck" with for the day? If so, this article is especially for you.

There was a large event that I did not want to attend. Trying to think of excuses to get out of going, I had already set in my mind that it was going to be a miserable experience. Finally, I sat myself down and gave myself a "talking-to." I realized that I was the creator of my own misery, and I needed to change my frame of mind. I decided to go on a "negativity fast."

I vowed not to utter a single complaint or negative word about anyone I was going to see at the event for thirty days. Every time I started to be anxious about our time together, I brought up each person's face and applied Hoʻoponopono, an ancient Hawaiian practice of forgiveness. If you're not familiar with Hoʻoponopono, you simply visualize the person you are having difficulties with and repeat the mantra, "I'm sorry. Please forgive me. I love you. Thank you." That's it.

It worked. Not only was the occasion a happy, fun day, but later when I saw a couple of the people I had been forgiving, they greeted me warmly with hugs and smiles. All is now good between us.

Do you have people in your life that irritate you or you find unpleasant to be around? Try this negativity fast, coupled with Ho'oponopono. I'd love to hear your experiences with this fantastic practice.

PS - Don't let others live "rent free" in your head. The stress is affecting you much more than it is affecting them.

Week 26: The Greatest Danger Lies Not in Setting Your Aim too High

"The greatest danger lies not in setting your aim too high and falling short: but on setting your aim too low and achieving your mark."

Michelangelo

Think about the goals that you have set recently. Do you think those goals are attainable? If so, you may be setting the bar too low.

In his book, *The Science of Getting Rich*, Wallace Wattles shares the story of a student's introduction to the law of attraction. He was told to get a clear picture in his mind of what he wanted and start believing he could have it. Being a reasonable man, he wanted a new rug and a stove for his modest home. He received both in a very short period and realized that he had not asked for enough. He then set about raising his expectations and was able to furnish his house to his fully desired state.

Jim used this same strategy and shared, "This is how I got to my current big hairy audacious revenue goal. I'm not there yet, but I'm a HELLUVA lot closer than I was two years ago because that goal is always present and alive."

Today, get out your goal list, take a look at what you've written down. Now double it. (Yes, I heard that gasp of breath.) Expect more of yourself and you may be surprised at how much more you can achieve than you thought possible.

PS - When you reach for the stars; you may end up "just" hitting the moon.

Week 27: Understanding the Reality of the Everyday

"To achieve excellence, we must first understand the reality of the every day, with all its demands and potential frustrations."
Mihaly Csikszentmihalyi

Are you exactly where you want to be right now? Have you reached the pinnacle of your professional pursuits? If so, you can stop reading now; this message is not for you.

Whew, you're still reading. It's true, life happens. According to one commercial, "Life comes at you fast." We think about our dreams and goals and how wonderful life is going to be when we finally have all that we desire. However, it's important that we also learn to enjoy the ride.

Do you see yourself as a number one New York Times best-selling author, but yet you haven't sat down to write the awesome book that's inside of you? So what. Write a blog post, an article, or a journal entry. Start to get the words that are inside of you written down on paper and little by little your book will take shape.

Do you dream of landing a large client who is going to help you exceedingly surpass your financial goals for the year? Pick up the phone. Attend a networking event. Ask for an introduction to somebody that may know someone else. Sometimes the people that you least expect to help you can offer you amazing connections that eventually get you exactly to where you want to be.

Every day, try to be 1% better than you were yesterday. Compete only with yourself and celebrate the little victories along your journey. You are already excellent, and every day you grow more so.

PS - Life is short, eat dessert first.

Week 28: Good Works are Links That Form a Chain of Love

"Good works are links that form a chain of love." No matter how small the act--even a smile given honestly--can bring positivity into the life of another."

Mother Teresa of Calcutta

Since December of 1984, Dick Clough and his "Tour of Good Cheer" have been distributing clothing, blankets, backpacks and toys to needy kids, and homeless men, women, children, and families. I have worked with the tour since 2009, and I have witnessed the difference that it makes.

People on the tour kindly acknowledge those whom they bring these gifts. Dick and his elves go the extra mile in making the recipient feel special, letting each know that we care about making the holiday season a little brighter. It's a magical night for the beneficiaries, who receive the warmth of the clothing as well as the warmth in the way the elves treat them. It's also a miraculous night for all the volunteers on the tour, and the energy is palatable. Even after almost twelve hours of work, the liveliness and spirit aboard the bus are still going strong.

Studies show that people who participate in any kind of volunteer work on a regular basis experience lower mortality rates, greater functional ability, and lower rates of depression later in life than those who do not. When we come to realize the number of people who are less fortunate than we are, we learn that we can serve others and ourselves in the process. It all starts with a smile.

Find an organization that has a special place in your heart, and look for ways that you can support them today.

PS - Check out The Tour of Good Cheer on Facebook to see the videos from the last few years.

Week 29: It's Always Too Early to Quit

"It's always too early to quit."

Norman Vincent Peale

In whatever business you are in right now, think about the people who are the most successful doing what you do. Before you start negatively comparing yourself to these people, ask yourself a couple of questions: "How long have they been in the industry?", "What hurdles have they overcome?", "What are they doing that's different from everyone else?"

Often it simply pays to be the last one standing. People who have been successful over the long haul have battled self-doubt, overcome obstacles, and persisted despite downturns in the economy. They kept going, even when it was hard.

I once debated with a friend of mine who insisted that not everyone could make it in their chosen profession. She contended that sometimes people have no choice but to give up. I countered with the fact that you ALWAYS have a choice. You can choose to go back to school while everyone else is watching TV. You can decide to work towards your dream while your friends want to play. You can strive to be just a little better today than you were yesterday when everyone else chooses to stagnate.

When you look at the most successful people you know, remember that they paid a significant price for their achievements. You always have a choice. If quitting is not an option, you will succeed - even if it's not in exactly the way that you initially imagined it would be.

PS - Listen to your heart, take the necessary action, DON'T QUIT, and you will achieve the success you seek.

Week 30: Appreciate what you have

"What if you gave someone a gift, and they neglected to thank you for it? Would you be likely to give them another? Life is the same way. In order to attract more of the blessings that life has to offer, you must truly appreciate what you already have."

Ralph Marston

Let's say, just for giggles, that you are sitting in traffic and another car is trying to merge. You slow down to let them cut in, and they don't so much as give you a wave. How do you feel? Are you going to be as ready and willing to let the next person merge in front of you?

Probably not.

How many times have you been the person who didn't wave? Little courtesies make life better.

It's essential to acknowledge the world around us when we are having a bad day. Isn't it true that when we concentrate on our little miseries, things seem to get worse? There's a snowball effect that is hard to define. Our thoughts can either work for us or against us.

Next time you are having a bad day, or a sad moment, pause and come up with one good thing that you have in your life right now - even if the only thing you can think of is oxygen. No matter how bad you feel, there is always going to be someone who is worse off than you.

Strive to make all your personal interactions positive; you have no idea the snowball effect YOU can have to make someone else's day.

PS - Don't forget to wave in traffic. You and the person you waved to will get to your destinations in a much happier state of mind.

Week 31: Life's "Calculator Carriers"

"The power of our minds to dream, to imagine and to create visions is one of our greatest and most important gifts. For out of the realm of the imagined can come the ideas we can use to create everything from a work of art to a life-changing discovery."

Morgan Simone

We all know the importance of having a dream. Think about the number of times you let someone else dash your dreams. Did you continue to pursue your goals, or did you try to find one that was more "realistic?"

An associate and I were discussing my aspirations for my speaking career. When I shared with her what I wanted to accomplish, she quickly brought out a calculator and proceeded to tell me how naive I was being for having such lofty goals. Instead of being sucked up into this negativity, I changed the subject, and we moved on. By choosing to ignore her, I allowed myself to protect my dream.

We want to see the highest and best for ourselves, but we have to deal with that little voice inside our heads asking, "What makes you so remarkable?

PLEASE KNOW THIS: You are remarkable. Your dreams count. You WILL exceed your wildest expectations by believing in yourself and taking requisite action towards your goal. If you have naysayers and calculator-carriers in your life, minimize your contact with them. Surround yourself with people who have lofty dreams of their own and support each other. The people you surround yourself with make all the difference.

PS - We all have the same 24 hours in our day. Choose to use your time wisely by scheduling time with the most positive people you know

Week 32: Risk Anything!

"Risk! Risk anything! Care no more for the opinion of others, for those voices. Do the hardest thing on earth for you. Act for yourself. Face the truth."

Katherine Mansfield

The universal truth about opinions is that we all have them. The problem is that we become so focused on our perception of the situation that we don't take into consideration that there truly are two sides to every story.

When you are pursuing your life's dreams, you may find that your friends and family don't understand what you're doing, and subsequently don't support your efforts. We get frustrated because we all want the acknowledgment and support of those we love. Remember, for all the stories that you are making up about them, they are making up their own stories about you.

If you choose to be an entrepreneur in a family of corporate 9-to-5'ers, chances are they will not understand. You see yourself with the freedom and flexibility of being your own boss while pursuing your passion; they may see you as someone that doesn't "work" for a living because you don't receive a regular paycheck.

If you choose to go back to school to get your degree and you associate with people who do not value higher education, they may see you as someone that wants to be "better" than them, and they may ridicule your efforts.

Choose to see the opinions of others for what they are - their own. You are not going to change them. Don't hold yourself back because of someone else's story, make up your own as you go along and create your own happy ending.

PS - Other people's opinions of you are none of your business.

Week 33: - Sixty Days from Now

"You simply will not be the same person two months from now after consciously giving thanks, each day for the abundance that exists in your life. And you will have set in motion an ancient spiritual law: the more you have and are grateful for, the more will be given you."

Sarah Ban Breathnach

This quote shares the unequivocal truth of the power behind the gratitude journal. If you are not already keeping track of three to five things every day for which you are grateful, please start today. You will not be the same person two months from now as you are today.

One of the questions that I get asked most when it comes to a Gratitude Journal is, "Does it have to be something different every day?" The answer is 'yes' and 'no.' You want to challenge yourself to be grateful for as many things as you possibly can each day because it makes you aware of the many blessings you have. However, you don't want to discount the constants in your life that you want to acknowledge.

For example, I am grateful every day for my hubby. I don't necessarily write that every day, because I have much more to write about, but he shows up on the list on a pretty regular basis, believe me. I make sure to add details as far as what I appreciate about Scott. I may write, "I am grateful that Scott and I had a fun night playing Scrabble last night." On the next day, my entry may be, "I am lucky to have a husband that loves and supports me in all of my ventures." As long as you can get to experience the feeling of gratefulness, you're on the right track.

Take a moment right now; grab a pen and a piece of paper and write down three to five things for which you are grateful. Do this every day for the next 60 days and let me know how you feel.

PS - Expressing gratitude every day, keeps the blues away.

Week 34: The Best Minute

"The best minute you spend is the one you invest in people."
Ken Blanchard

You never know how the people you meet will make a difference in your life. A few years ago, I met a woman while networking. We exchanged cards and scheduled to meet for coffee. I didn't know what we had in common, but I thought she was very nice, and I wanted to get to know her better.

During our conversation, we talked about social media. She was just starting to get into it and was struggling with what she should do. I shared with her several of the best tips that I had discovered in my social media exploration. Surprised, she asked, "Why are you giving me all of this information without charging me for it?"

I was a taken aback, as I was merely sharing knowledge that I thought she would find helpful. She then asked me what she could do to help me. I told her that if she knew of any organizations that were hiring speakers, I'd love to make the connection. That statement led to three speaking engagements that directly resulted in three of my biggest clients.

If I had blown her off because I didn't see any value in making the connection, my business would not be where it is today. When you spend time with people, look first for ways that you can be of service to them. Invest in them and the payoff may be bigger than you can imagine.

What can you do today to be a resource for the people that you meet?

PS - By making a difference in the lives of others, they will make a difference for you.

Week 35: Be Nice to EVERYONE!

"Be nice to everyone you meet. Sooner or later they will show up again in your life."

Lisa Ryan

If I were to say to you, "It's a very small world," I'm sure you would agree. There no longer seems to be that famous "six degrees of separation," it feels more like two.

For many years, I rented a house across the street from a family that I affectionately nicknamed "the porch people." They were on their porch from the time I went to work in the morning until I went to bed at night, or so it seemed. I never got to know these people; and a casual wave and saying "Hi," was about as deep as our relationship ever got.

Many years later, I was on the golf course. Since I was golfing alone, the starter teamed me up with a couple that was going out at the same time. They were very nice, and we conversed through our nine holes together. The conversation came down to, "Where do you live?" Both said they were from Garfield Heights. Funny, that's where I used to live. We compared notes, and I found that the guy was the son of "the porch lady." I remembered seeing him and waving to him on several occasions. On one hand, I felt good because it was always a friendly wave, but I also felt bad because it never went any deeper. After reestablishing the contact, we stayed in touch, and a friendship developed.

This incident was a powerful reminder that people come into our lives for a reason, a season, or a lifetime. No matter what the reason is, it's always best to err on the side of being nice.

PS - A smile, a wave, or a kind word is all it takes to open the door for a relationship now or at some point in the future.

Week 36: Take a Risk - and Act

"Often the difference between a successful person and a failure is not one has better abilities or ideas, but the courage that one has to bet on one's ideas, to take a calculated risk - and to act. "

Andre Malraux

It was the third interview for a medical sales position that I desperately wanted. The interview started off well enough, but soon took a dramatic turn for the worse. It wasn't looking good.

Having nothing to lose, I asked the interviewer what the problem was. He told me that I did not have the experience that they needed for the position. At that moment, I realized I could play nice, or I could go for it. After all, if I was going to burn a bridge, I might as well throw some gasoline on it.

With a head bob and a finger point, I let him know that I had EXACTLY the expertise that he needed for this position. I gave him concrete examples of each key point where he felt my credential were lacking. The interview ended a few minutes later, and I walked out without the offer. However, on the way to the airport, my new boss contacted me and offered me my dream position, which I accepted on the spot.

Risking it all led to a job I held for the next seven years.

When you know something is right; sometimes you have to take a risk and ACT upon your instincts. What will you go for today?

PS - Maybe a head bob and finger point is NOT the best gesture you can make to a potential employer, but standing your ground with absolute certainty is.

Week 37: Creating a Vision for Tomorrow

"Gratitude makes sense of our past, brings peace for today, and creates a vision for tomorrow."

Author Unknown

How many times have you thought, "If I only knew then what I know now"? Stop, pause and be grateful that you now have this knowledge. Once you reflect, you realize that everything that happened made you into the person you are today.

If you could go back in time, what would you change? Would you go to your prom even if you didn't like high school? Would you have had children even though you didn't have a maternal bone in your body? Would you have gone to college right after high school? Every decision you make leads to a chain of circumstances that directly affect your outcomes.

Frankly, I don't know if going to my high school prom would have changed the way my life turned out. I do know that my decisions not to have children and not to take the traditional route for college have profoundly impacted my life. Back then I wasn't sure. Now I understand.

Don't try to figure out everything that is going on in your life. Be grateful for the times you've had, the times you are having, and the times that you will have. It all comes together if you let it.

PS - You are an incredible person. You have your past to thank, your present to enjoy, and your future to look forward to with glee.

Week 38: Be Careful What You Wish For

"Be careful what you wish for, you just might get it."
Unknown

Here's a cautionary tale from Diane, that reminds us of just how powerful we are: "I love chocolate and admittedly consider myself a chocoholic. I am very healthy, eat organically, antibiotic free chicken, and work out every day. I consider myself to be the picture of health, within reason. Three times this month someone offered me their chocolate dessert saying they were allergic and got migraines from it. Jokingly I said each time, 'I wish I was allergic to chocolate so that I wouldn't want it all the time!"

"Two days ago I received test results and am allergic to gluten, eggs, and soy. I've had to cut my food intake substantially as soy is in chocolate, ketchup, canned tuna, canned soups, nearly everything as an inexpensive food filler. Gluten is in salad dressing and millions of other products as a thickener, not to mention bread, cookies, cereals and cakes. Eggs are eggs, and I will miss them.

"After a day of transition toward acceptance, I can now say that I am grateful for the knowledge of what my allergens are, and look forward to being truly healthy. I have moved to another level of gratitude and am so grateful not to be allergic to milk products, so I can still have hormone free fat free milk in my coffee! Life is good."

Remember - YOU ARE POWERFUL! You can use the power of your mind to create positive things in your life, or not. It's up to you.

PS - But whatever you get, make the best of it!

Week 39: Week - Nothing Can Stop You

"Nothing can stop the man with the right mental attitude from achieving his goal; nothing on earth can help the man with the wrong mental attitude."

Thomas Jefferson

In the movie, "The Gratitude Experiment," Mary Morrissey talks about the annual fires in California. One year a deadly fire raged through an exclusive neighborhood, and many people lost their multi-million dollar homes. Of course, reporters were on site, interviewing people who were surveying the complete destruction of what once was their home. One couple was in front of their home, holding each other and sobbing uncontrollably. When the reporter asked them about their situation, the woman said, "We lost everything, how could this happen to use? We have nothing left."

On the same day, same neighborhood, another couple was asked about how they were handling the loss of their home. The woman replied, "We are so grateful that everyone got out safe. We are lucky to be here and together. We have everything we need."

Same story, different attitude. Who do you think get their life back together more quickly after the devastation?

You always have a choice of how you look at a situation. No matter the circumstances, when you look for something positive, you will ALWAYS find it. What do you need to change your perception of right now?

PS - You can always replace material possessions. The people that we love and the values that we have cannot - that's why they reside in our heart.

Week 40: The Real Winner in Life

"The real winners in life are the people who look at every situation with an expectation that they can make it work or make it better."

Barbara Pletcher

Think about your all-time favorite teacher. In many cases, your teachers made an impact on your life that far outlasted your education. My sixth-grade teacher, Sister Stephanie was the best teacher ever. Memories of her still make me smile. Her favorite joke was, "How do you make holy water?" Answer: "You boil the hell out of it." At a time when we spelled "hell" by saying "H-E- double toothpicks," we loved hearing a nun use a naughty word.

Sister Stephanie's unique feature was her wooden leg. She might have lost her leg, but she never lost her humor. Whenever someone said, "Knock on wood," she would simply tap on her leg. Because of her, I learned not to take life so seriously.

Sister Stephanie was my hero because she made every situation better in school. Even though she had a stroke and had to leave our school halfway through the year, I kept in touch with her. She was determined not to let a mere stroke keep her down, so she enrolled in a writing course. Years later she sent me a story that she wrote with me cast as the main character. She had me penned as a gum-chewing wise-cracking, teenager, with a big smile and a loud laugh. Yep, she nailed it.

What can you do today to make something better for yourself or someone else? Now that you've thought of it, the next step is to take the steps and do it.

PS - Who is your Sister Stephanie? Take a minute a silently thank her (or him).

Week 41: Nothing is Good or Bad

"Nothing is good or bad but thinking it makes it so."
Shakespeare

International travel can be a nightmare. Last time I flew to Calgary, the customs agent interrogated me for forty-five minutes about my purpose for visiting their country. I mistakenly handed her my Blackberry so she could see my flight information and she scrolled through my emails for twenty minutes, trying to find "evidence" against me.

Fast forward two and a half years: I'm flying into Calgary again and anxious about customs. I soon realized that if I were to keep thinking those thoughts, customs would once again be horrible. I considered the differences for my trip - I was there for a week instead of three days. I had all my paperwork in order, and printed documentation for the movie premiere and workshops I was going to attend. I correctly declared my CDs that I was giving away in the VIP "Swag Bags." I had done all the right things for this trip, and I felt better about it.

Going through customs was a breeze. When I told the agent I was coming into Canada to attend a movie premiere, and take a workshop, he asked about the premiere. When I showed him the flyer and the fact that

I was in the film, he lit up. He congratulated me, wished me success and sent me on my way. Easy peasy.

If you have something coming up that you're dreading, how can you choose to see the situation differently? You may be pleasantly surprised by the result.

PS - When you're filled with dread, you give off a vibration that others sense. Change your attitude, change your vibe.

Week 42: A First Rate Version of Yourself

"Always be a first-rate version of yourself, instead of a second-rate version of somebody else."

Judy Garland

What happens when you get to meet one of your "bucket list" people? While in Calgary, I had the honor of picking up Dr. John Demartini for the red carpet premiere of The Gratitude Experiment movie. I was nervous, as Dr. Demartini was a person I had wanted to meet for a long time. His book, *Count Your Blessings*, was one of the first books I discovered when I started studying gratitude, and I've been a fan ever since.

The first thing I noticed about him was his incredible vocabulary. Wow! He oozed knowledge and expertise - I was intimidated. Then I figured that I could try to use big words and be considered more intellectual, or I could just be me, in my active, star-struck, excitable state. I chose the latter, and I'm glad I did.

When you meet someone for the first time, they are going to like you, dislike you or be neutral. In many cases, that person will automatically like you because you remind them of someone they like, or they will dislike you because you remind them of someone you dislike. Since you don't have a lot of control over either situation, why not just be yourself? It's a lot easier to remember the truth of who you are, rather than all of the "cool stuff" you had to make up.

PS - Be yourself, everyone else is taken.

Week 43: Concentrate on the Good

"If you concentrate on finding whatever is good in every situation, you will discover that your life will suddenly be filled with gratitude, a feeling that nurtures the soul."

Rabbi Harold Kushner

A couple of months before my thirtieth birthday, I was struggling with a deep depression. I was comparing my life in a very unfavorable way to all of my friends. They were all married, had beautiful houses, drove nice cars and had cute kids. I, on the other hand, was dating Mr. "Right-Now," renting a house, leasing a car, and living with my four cats (a recipe for dating disaster).

I needed to get out of my funk, so I asked myself the question, "What is GOOD about my situation?" It took a while, but it finally dawned on me: "Wait a minute –I don't own a house, I don't have kids, I don't own a car, and I have no husband. These are the BEST times of my life! I am in control of my life – I can do what I want, whenever I want, and I don't have to answer to anyone. Life is good!"

Within three months of my attitude adjustment, the love of my life, Scott, showed up. If I had not cleared the space for him – breaking up with Mr. Right-Now, and appreciating where I was in my life; it might not have happened. We married in April of 1996, and I am profoundly grateful every day for him. In what areas of your life would it be helpful for you to accept what you have, the way it is, and look for the good in it?

PS - When you clear your resentment, envy, and/or disappointment, you open the space for the people, events, and circumstances that you desire to come into your life.

Week 44: Self-Help versus Shelf-Help

"Formal education will make you a living; self-education will make you a fortune. "

Jim Rohn

What have you learned today? The self-development industry is a HUGE industry, bringing in billions of dollars each year. Of course, it would be interesting to find out how many of those books, videos, audio programs, etc. are actually read, watched or listened to. Even more fascinating would be the percentage of these products people act upon. Inaction is when self-help becomes SHELF-help.

How often do you acquire new knowledge? Daily, weekly or are you an "I-haven't-pick-up-a-book-since-college" person? As a book junkie, I love information. I am grateful for the opportunity to hold books in my hand. I love sitting on the couch, reading with a kitty on my lap. Or, thankfully, I can kill two birds with one stone by reading while on the treadmill. When attending seminars and workshops, nothing makes my day better than having the opportunity to bring that presenter home with me in the form of their products. Life is great when we share what we know, and we take the time to learn from others.

Although it's easy to veg out in front of the television, it may interest you to know that watching TV uses as many brain cells as sleeping. (Yes, even if you're watching the History Channel.)

Don't like to speak in public? Join Toastmasters. Think you can't figure out social media? Take a class. Believe that you don't have time to go to school? Visit www.coursera.com and find a variety of online classes from world-renowned universities you can take for free.

When you're increasing your skills, you're growing. When you stop growing, your skills decrease, your motivation wanes, your passion fades. Challenge yourself to cultivate new talents and abilities. Get outside your comfort zone and take on something different. You may surprise yourself and renew your zest for life.

PS - Defy your fears and experience the rewards of success.

Week 45: Be grateful for your problems

"The hardest arithmetic to master is that which enables us to count our blessings."

Eric Hoffer

When our seventeen-year-old cat, Tigger died, it was tough for both us, but particularly for my husband, Scott. Tigger was his baby, and he missed her terribly. After several months of grieving, Scott was ready to adopt a new kitten.

We visited a local shelter and Scott picked up a tiny, scrawny gray kitten who weighed a mere 2.6 pounds. As he held her, not only did she start purring, she tried climbing onto his shoulder, exactly like Tigger used to do. This tiny angel won Scott's heart, and Simba came home with us.

Unfortunately, Simba had just about every disease in the book. She was malnourished, had roundworms, an upper respiratory infection, goopy eyes, and some kind of skin "funk." Needless to say, Simba was a very expensive kitty very quickly.

We could have counted the money we spent on Simba and complained about it. Instead, we focused on the blessings and joy she brought to our home. She's now healthy it's a pleasure to be around kitten energy again.

Next time you open your mouth to complain about something, see if you can find one good thing about the situation. Express your appreciation for it, even if it's in your head (of course, its better out loud.) By changing your focus, you will discover that you can always find something good, even if's just a tiny, scrawny little thing.

PS - The math in the checkbook is not nearly as important as the arithmetic of the heart.

Week 46: Asking for What You Want

"Ask, and it shall be given you; seek and you shall find; knock, and it shall be opened to you. For everyone who asks, receives; and he who seeks, finds; and to him who knocks, it shall be opened."

Matthew: 7:7, 7:8

Barb shares the power of asking for what you want. "My daughter and I went to the mall and had just a great time! When we got home that night, she cried, 'Mommy, I can't find my purse." I said, 'It's okay honey, it is only a purse.' She explained, 'No mommy, you don't understand. It had ALL my money and my gift cards in it.'

"I felt bad, but there was nothing I could do for her other than to say I would call the mall in the morning to see if someone turned it in. I gave her a big hug and said that whatever the outcome, at least she learned something. Even though she felt horrible, I was grateful that it was only money. I released the result and felt a sense of peace come over me.

The next day, I called the mall, and they did not have it. I felt an urge to call the last store we were in, and they had her purse! Yea! "

Sometimes we confuse asking with begging. Barb's story teaches us to ask for what we want (the return of the bag) and to be okay with the outcome - whatever it is. If you are begging for a particular result, let it go. Ask once for what you want to receive. Believe that your highest and best will come to you, and you'll receive the gifts of knowledge, understanding, and experience.

PS - If you don't open the door when opportunity knocks, when will you open it?

Week 47: - Life's Free Gifts

"When we are grateful, we appreciate life's free gifts: friendship and solitude; movement and rest; Nature's Bounty and her spare winter introversion; our own alternating sonata movements of joy, sorrow, and joy's resurgence. Through this appreciation, we find contentment."

Unknown

While visiting Banff, in the Canadian Rockies, I had the opportunity to summit Sulphur Mountain (my first summit!). The beauty and majesty of standing on that mountaintop brought tears to my eyes. What a marvelous place!

Dale shares his thoughts on the beauty of nature. "I do find wonder and awe in nature. The other night I had my telescope on the moon, and I could see the craters and mountains. It's hard to believe that we had men walking up there! I am grateful we have air and fresh water. It's amazing that of all the planets in our solar system, Earth is the only one that can support our humanity. We should be grateful for our uniqueness."

You don't need to have massive manifestations happen in your life to express sincere appreciation. Take a moment today to appreciate the world around you - the flora, the fauna, the fresh air. You'll be amazed by the bounty that surrounds all of us. What's your favorite part of nature? Write it down and capture the moment.

PS - Take a mini-vacation in the great outdoors today. Even if it's just standing in your backyard - appreciate the beauty that envelops you.

Week 48: Sincere Words of Praise

"As I express my gratitude, I become more deeply aware of it. And the greater my awareness, the greater my need to express it. What happens here is a spiraling ascent, a process of growth in ever expanding circles around a steady center."

David Steindl-Rast

A long-time Gratitude Thought for the Week reader shares how her gratitude practice gave her the strength her to deal with a tough life situation, "Our son took a horrible drunken fall, resulting in traumatic brain injuries, aspirated vomit, and time in the ICU. He was on life support for three weeks and then spent two weeks in rehab to relearn everything.

"We were blown away by the choices he was making in his private life. However, had it not been FOR the accident, we would have never known of the things he was getting into. He surely would have died (and nearly did in the hospital). We are grateful we found out; grateful he survived and is pretty much fully intact; and grateful for his straight A's and razor-focus performance in college. Although he still has some thought process issues, impulsivity, lack of smell, few friends, and mood issues, we know in our hearts that he is a walking miracle."

It is the practice of gratitude that builds your "gratitude muscle" and gives you the ability to find gratefulness when life hands you a significant challenge. When you consciously look for people, events, and circumstances to appreciate, your life positively changes on every level.

PS - Start today, with whatever you have and where ever you are. If you are finding it difficult to find things in your life to be thankful for, it's even more important that you do so. Are you breathing? Walking? Reading? Start there.

Week 49: Leaving the World a Better Place

"To laugh often and much; to win the respect of intelligent people and the affection of children...to leave the world a better place...to know even one life has breathed easier because you have lived. This is to have succeeded."

Ralph Waldo Emerson

Avaria shares a compelling story of what real success is. "Life for me living in the Caribbean is splendid. I remember having big dreams of living overseas and studying abroad, but I opted to stay here and be closer to my family. I eventually got a job, although not my perfect job, it pays the bills and allows me flexibility. At this job, I met my best friend, Jonathan. He was charismatic, open and became part of my family. He was there for every major aspect of my life, and I lost him in a vehicular accident in July 2011.

"He was killed on his way to work. I remember the sick feeling I had - it felt like I lost a part of myself. After a time, I decided to shift my thinking to see this situation for what it was. After all, God has been good to me. I still have days when I just cry, but I am also grateful. Jonathan taught me love, respect, the importance to remain humble and honest and most importantly to love. Gratitude is the attitude. I feel like I won a lottery, that's how amazing I feel."

Looking back on the tragedies that have taken place in your life, isn't it true that you often discover that these incidents transformed you into the person that you are today? Everything happens for a reason, and although it doesn't always make sense at the time, sooner or later the significance of that event will be revealed.

PS - I'm not saying that it will always be easy or painful, but finding gratitude in the situation makes it simpler and less painful.

Week 50: Who You Are and Who You May Be

"We know what we are, but not what we may be."
William Shakespeare

You always remember your first job. I was a server at Coney Island at Randall Park Mall. It was not a great job, but I was 14, and they didn't care that I was underage. (Plus, I wanted money to go shopping.) The food was bad, the tips were minimal, and management seemed to take glee in berating the staff in front of customers. Even at my tender age, I knew that this wasn't where I wanted to be.

On a particularly hectic Saturday afternoon, while the managers were yelling get the waitresses, the waitresses were slinging food at the customers, and the customers were vowing never to come back, I reached my tipping point (no pun intended). I walked out. The only other thing that I remember about that day is the owner of the restaurant following me up the escalator screaming at me and demanding when I would return my polyester brown, permanently smelly, uniform. It was funny, even back then.

Since that time, I have never taken a job in which I've had to "settle." Not all of my jobs have worked out, or ended up being perfect for me, but they were fine at the time that I took them.

Are you doing what you love right now or are you settling for what life hands you? Remember, nature abhors a vacuum, so when you create the space for what you want to do, letting something else go may be the order of the day.

PS - From Coney Island to a career in sales, to an entrepreneur -it's been an exciting ride. Is your path helping you discover who you are?

Week 51: Regretting the Things You Haven't Done

"You'll seldom experience regret for anything that you've done. It is what you haven't done that will torment you. The message, therefore, is clear. Do it! Develop an appreciation for the present moment. Seize every second of your life and savor it. Using them up in any self-defeating ways means you've lost them forever."

Wayne Dyer

Recently, a friend and I were discussing what one thing we wished we would have done in our lives. What popped into my mind was the fact that I didn't go to college right out of high school. Now remember, not only was college not an option for me because of my family's financial situation, I never thought about going. I didn't have friends that were going to college, I didn't know anything about college, and therefore I just went to work instead.

Several years out of high school, I began the journey to achieve my college education and fourteen years later completed an MBA. Although I think that I might have enjoyed the college experience: having sorority sisters, living away from home amongst other college students, and attending "Animal House"-type frat parties, I also know that my life would've turned out completely differently.

So when it all comes down to it, it's no longer a regret. I'm glad I accepted a part-time job teaching aerobics at Scandinavian Health Club. I'm thrilled that it was at Bally's where I developed some of my closest friendships, and I met my wonderful husband, Scott. I'm grateful that after a rough start, I built a successful career. And I'm so thankful for my current life as an entrepreneur. It doesn't get any better than this!

Starting now, if there's something in your life that you want to do, go for it. You'll only regret the things you don't do. However, if there's something in your past that you didn't do, and now you regret it, think about all the things that happened BECAUSE you didn't do it. Chances are good that things turned out exactly the way they were supposed to.

PS - I always wanted to jump out of an airplane before I die, just not IMMEDIATELY before I die! :-)

Week 52: Escaping the Pressures of Mainstream Media

"Discover the fulfillment of intimate relationships with flesh-and-blood neighbors and teammates in concrete place and time, and we escape the pressure of mainstream media to channel intimacy only as a virtual embrace."

Jose Panate-Aceves and John Hayes

Nancy shares her neighborly experience, "I got divorced eight years ago. The house we lived in is rather large and has a decent sized yard. My co-workers thought that I should sell my house and downsize to a smaller place. Their opinion was that "It was just a house." I did not sell and here is the reason why:

"I have some of the best neighbors anyone could have. My best friend lives three doors up, and there are six or seven other friends that, if I needed something, no matter what it would be, I could call them, and one of them would help me. The support system we have among that small group is wonderful! So, to me, it was not "just a house" it was much more than that.

"I am very grateful for my neighborhood. (Of course, we have those couple neighbors that we all wish would move out, but all neighborhoods have those.)"

Neighborhoods host a wide variety of people, belief systems, and lifestyles. Today make it a goal to concentrate on what's right about your community instead of nit-picking about the little annoyances. If there are people you'd like to get to know better, invite them over for a cup of coffee, or bring over some fresh bakery. Friendships take a while to grow and form, and when you can keep them close to home, you'll make for a much happier homestead.

When you know your neighbors, you not only create a stronger community, you create a safer place to live as everyone looks out for everyone else. Don't know your neighbors well? Find a reason to get together and let the friendship begin!

PS - Fresh baked cookies, a smile and wave, a small get-together - no reason is too little to strike up a conversation.

Congratulations!

You have finished the *52 More Weeks of Gratitude*. When you consider the many ways you can express your appreciation, I hope you were able to add some new ideas to your list. Taking just a few minutes each day in thankfulness makes all the difference in your perception of life.

My programs focus on the power of gratitude in business and in life. When you SHOW appreciation, it transforms your SELF or your life perspective. It improves your HEALTH by offering the benefits a stronger heart and more efficient immune system. It strengthens your relationships with OTHERS as you consciously express your thankfulness to your loved ones regularly. It magnifies your WEALTH, personally and professional, as you learn to focus on the good things you have in your life.

Are you ready to start your daily gratitude practice now?

Be Thankful

Be thankful that you don't already have everything you desire,
If you did, what would there be to look forward to?
Be thankful when you don't know something
For it gives you the opportunity to learn.
Be thankful for the difficult times.
During those times you grow.
Be thankful for your limitations
Because they give you opportunities for improvement.
Be thankful for each new challenge
Because it will build your strength and character.
Be thankful for your mistakes
They will teach you valuable lessons.
Be thankful when you're tired and weary
Because it means you've made a difference.
It is easy to be thankful for the good things.
A life of rich fulfillment comes to those who are
also thankful for the setbacks.

GRATITUDE can turn a negative into a positive.
Find a way to be thankful for your troubles
and they can become your blessings.

Author Unknown

About Lisa Ryan

I discovered the power of gratitude in 2009 after attending a four-day intensive workshop with friends. We had an amazing experience at the seminar and wanted to keep the energy we experienced flowing forward. We opened up a Facebook thread and shared three things that we were grateful for every day. We held each other accountable for this daily practice.

This simple practice changed my life. From my medical sales position, to my relationship with my husband, I noticed the changes within a very short period. The only action I could attribute these changes to was my daily practice of gratitude.

I began to research what I experiencing by reading white papers, reports, books and attending countless programs. I knew that this knowledge was to become my mission – to change the world, one "thank you" at a time.

As Founder and Chief Appreciation Strategist at Grategy®, I work with corporations, associations, and non-profits to keep their top talent and best clients from becoming someone else's. Through my Grategy® programs, audiences realize how they can use the power of appreciation to develop stronger relationships, improve their health and increase profits by creating a culture of appreciation.

To learn more about Grategy® or to book me for your next event, please visit www.grategy.com. You can also contact me at lisa@grategy.com.

Thank you, I appreciate you!

Other Books / Film from Lisa Ryan:

The Upside of Down Times: Discovering the Power of Gratitude

Uncover four areas in your life that can be transformed by using the power of appreciation. Entertaining, inspiring and includes plenty of activities so you can get started right away.

Express Gratitude, Experience Good: Your Daily Gratitude Journal

Keep track of your daily gratitudes and learn about the experiences of others who participated in the "Thirty Day Gratitude Challenge"

52 Weeks of Gratitude: Transformation Through Appreciation

A compilation of Lisa Ryan's first year of "Gratitude Thought for the Week" Now available in e-book and print.

From Afraid to Speak to Paid to Speak: How Overcoming Public Speaking Anxiety Boosts your Confidence and Career (Kindle and print)

Learn to minimize your fear of public speaking, develop your speech and put together a plan to deliver it.

Thank You Notes: Your 30 Days of Gratitude Workbook

Take the challenge. For the next 30 days, discover all the ways you can harness the power of gratitude

The Verbal Hug (Kindle only)

Filled with 101 unique ways to share your appreciation with others.

Keeper of the Keys: Taking the Hell Out of Self-Help **(film)** http://lisaryanonline.com

Laid off from his job, his house in foreclosure, his engagement broken, Michael Walden was having a bad day. This film follows Michael's incredible journey to finding the keys to a happy and successful life. Also starring Jack Canfield (Chicken Soup for the Soul), Marci Shimoff (The Secret) and John Gray (Men are from Mars.)

Let's Keep in Touch

Questions for the Author?

Email Lisa Ryan at lisa@grategy.com

Want to receive Lisa Ryan's "Gratitude Thought for the Week?"

http://www.grategy.com

Before You Go…

Please share this book with your friends, family, or colleagues who can use a lift. To order in bulk, please contact me directly for pricing.

Also, I'd be honored if you'd post your thoughts about this book on social media as well as share a review of it on Amazon. Thank you!

Have fun,

Lisa